Kind Fire

ALSO BY BARRY HILL

The Schools (1977)
A Rim of Blue: Stories (1978)
Near the Refinery: a novella (1980)
Headlocks and Other Stories (1983)
The Best Picture: a novel (1988)
Raft: Poems 1983–1990 (1990)
Sitting In (1991)
Ghosting William Buckley: a poem (1993)
The Rock: Travelling to Uluru (1997)
The Inland Sea: Poems (2001)
Broken Song: T G H Strehlow and Aboriginal Possession (2002)
The Enduring Rip: A History of Queenscliffe (2004)
The War Sonnets (2007)
Necessity: Poems 1996–2006 (2007)
Four Lines East (2007)
As We Draw Ourselves (2008)
Lines for Birds (2011)
Naked Clay: Drawing from Lucian Freud (2012)
Peacemongers (2014)
Grass Hut Work (2016)
Reason & Lovelessness: Essays, encounters, reviews 1980–2017 (2018)
Eagerly We Burn: Selected Poems: 1980–2018 (2019)

KIND FIRE

BARRY HILL

ARCADIA

First published 2020 by ARCADIA
the general books' imprint of
Australian Scholarly Publishing Pty Ltd
7 Lt Lothian St Nth, North Melbourne, Victoria 3051

tel 03 9329 6963 / *fax* 03 9329 5452
aspic@ozemail.com.au / www.scholarly.info

ISBN: 978-1-925984-80-4

Cover design: Joe Hill

for Paul Kane

He wouldn't do a hand's turn
As long as he lived, she said.
So I had him cremated
Once he was dead.

He's been of more use since,
For you see, my dear,
These are his ashes

In the egg-timer here.

'Working at Last', HUGH MACDIARMID

Once wine gets into a poem's gut, wind and fire swell up,
And once a moon gets in, there's ice and snow everywhere,

Then before a single cup's dry, the poem's already done
Me chanting it out, startling heaven itself...

YANG WANG-LIE

CONTENTS

1

2

3

1

Kind Fire

i.m. Seamus Heaney

Not the digging of potatoes
but the forging of iron implements
produced those shoulders
and the biceps I pressed—
a little boy's hand on the father's bulge
a swelling roughly the same shape

as the hammer's head
I still have, along with his chisel
as thick as my wrist was thin.
Tools hand-made, part-time
in time stolen from the boss
at the Victorian Railways Erecting Shop—

one of the great sheds among many
in the long dry grass with the thistles
out past the Abattoirs
on the way to the back beach:
ribbed sand, soldier crabs, an oily creek
eels a bike ride from home

me sitting on the little padded seat
the iron-framed perch between his arms
near the handle bars
his breath a bellows on my neck
his kind fire always there
as he peddled me into the Southerly.

Beloved Historian at Home

For the late Hugh Stretton and Patsy Stretton

He cannot remember a line of his great works
or my name, but most days he locates his toothbrush.

And he can, still, turn to his wife
who finds him there in his well of love.

Two Poems to Songs

Crazy!

I stick my head out the back and call:
Let's go to the studio and play Patsy!

The spring grass is green, thickening as the fresias climb.
Who can forget her face, its glisten, the ruby-lipped shine?

You do not glance at the open studio door.
You barely look my way before breaking into the song yourself

caressing the petals of the sasanqua
warming the air with Butcher Bird chime

then pulling me in towards you because
I am your garden hose without an unkind

kink as I slip into something I hardly knew
I had in me: leaning against a deck post

I did a Pierrot, his beneath the moon mime
in *Les Enfants du Paradis* as you, with your own slow, high notes

curling up and around, smoking the garden and the song's longing
time put sanity beyond our happy blue reach.

Eventually, I came to ground, recovered something of myself.
In ravished yearning you sang on, and that was *beyond* fine.

Who needs YouTube?
Few of us are, finally, lost, and that's fine too.

I bet you could hear my own low-level, smothering croon
as I waited to recline at no cost, to love-fuck you by the compost.

Guilty!

Yes, baby, Ah bin drinkin
—Randy Newman

The bricks in this kitchen
were laid by a bloke a bit pissed

& blissed I am with her
in bare feet as she sings

Randy's song
Randy's unrepentant sorry song
right down into my throat.

One night— first time—
she dropped it into me neat.
A lingering kiss of legitimating misery.

Next time
she held the higher notes
and warbled what I sought

as approval
approval of all
I've been meaning to be—

with her, without her, before her—
on and off the road

coming and going
in and out of the cold
the promises and whisky and hope.

Her singing swells in me.
It revels in my snowy hair.
She sings

like a stream, like the Ganges
of all good things
in the wide forgiving world.

And I bet the fuck
she has been with him
or someone very like him

all the way to my door.

Sleeping with Lawrence

You are asleep, still, on this first morning of the year
and I am re-reading *Look, We Have Come Through*—
his sickly 'Wedlock', and also his 'New Heaven, New Earth'.

You are snoring, your face like that little bull he refers to.
I woke wrung out, as if I'd been walking
all night among crucifixes in the Alps.

I have my love of him to read him with
just as I have my love for you, you in your musical slumbers
the long sleeps that make you ever more mortal.

I have my love of his love of the death-swoon
just as I have my love of the raft that is you.
He would have himself rest between Frieda's breasts.

And I have you, awake or not, fretful or not, O
that never-ending nerviness he had as a young man?
He was a boy with the tendencies of an old man

one arriving to fuck with the way death sprouts
in a life, the loins ever cleansed, self-groomed
in the company of a mate, like a mountain lion—

some craggy self with a John the Baptist torso.
You'd think there was nothing else but sex and death.
Watching you asleep, splayed, my blood rises to your warmth

no matter what, and Lawrence offered his truths
with abandonment, was bravely able to set love and hate
down in the same bed, where else?

So bare one is on waking— like you, like me, us as we stood
in our sandals on their terrace at Taormino, with them
standing barefoot by the terracotta pots on the cool tiles

looking into their kitchen, their new heaven and
love produce from their new hearth. And you're lying here
the way they gardened fire and surrender—

the ginger-haired man and the straw-haired woman
downy hair on her neck, like your underarms.
When the sun comes in on you of a morning it becalms

the world, I won't have to calm you, or you me
you are the raft and the sail, such pluck you have, even while sleeping.
I might well, come to think of it, slip back into bed

and be on your loving arm, like Frieda's ample shoulders
as heavy as the earth he could press her into
the better to be darkened and reborn, in new earth—

not unlike, don't you think, the earth you helped your father work…
Lawrence would have loved you on a horse. Not to mention
the way you plonked, as a little girl, you wide bum on the fruit box

beside the dam— watching frog-spawn, yabby catching.
And Lawrence would have followed you into the long grass
where you lay still until the sheep arrived to surround you, circling in

because you had stretched out there, belonging
with the creatures of the earth, its stardust and excrement
everything implicated in everything else, alive or dead.

Some people, I know, dislike my directness as much as I love his.
I have seen you baulk at some things I say, sounding brutal
when tenderness drives me.

My words are dark, my heart is light like his, I tell you it is like his.
I wish you had grown up with him as I did on the lava plain.
Did I ever tell you I lived on a farm called *David Herbert?*

It had flowers, it had eagles. It had the crows
that fell like stones into your dam on the hot days.
I walked around naked in the heat— erect, proud, lizard-worshiping.

Even now, I read him feeling young, and old at the same time.
You with your sleeping sickness every new morning
presenting us with heavenly death, me with my lungs like his.

His lungs. In another era, I too would have died 'before my time.'
Time: breath did not really fail him. It is a myth that it did.
Words never ceased to rise into his throat like flying fish.

In his spaces without words, there was a whoosh of silver.
The same with your singing. Your music silvers everything.
In the dry dust you make perfume out of fresh rain.

He would have loved that.

The Glove

A friend
one who Pound would have called
    an old man with beautiful manners
        a Beethoven man
dwelling in the divine structures
    from the beginning
        to the end of his time
was telling me of his present, slow days
    of how his mornings
        some of his loveliest time is spent
        fingering…

I was at a loss.
    Poets have no word for what
        he was intimating….
Except perhaps to say—
    like choreography for hands
    like a dance of heart-mind or

    approaching a form of emptiness
    like touching fullness on the shoulder
        having it turn around…

Cross these out. Stay dumb. Just
    leave him be next time you meet.
Quietly imagine yourself
    slipping your own hand
        into a god's glove.

Conversation in a Heat Wave

For Godwin Bradbeer

We'd taken refuge, escaping the hot northerly
to be at ease near the door into his studio.
I could see a ravishing face, cool in its brooding light.
Too dark for her to live with, he told me.
So she brought her portrait back.

'Be ahead of all parting'— I almost cited Rilke, but fazed.
We were just knocking a few things around without saying
too much; we did not want, or need, to get pissed
there was still a lot to do, but the heat permitted a smiling question:
where/how was one's work to end, what was fucking next?

It was hard not to say something about the huge *Sexual Intercourse.*
It commanded a wall without moving—
a borrowing, an enlargement by permission of a Spaniard.
My friend spoke as if I should ignore it, and I did.
Then, as an act of trust, he went elsewhere to open a drawer

and rolled out the big cat, the start of a work to come.
Still not quite done...

The tail was slim, perhaps not snow-leopard enough.
If it was a tiger, its eye-socket was recessed
the hipbone still a gleam under the skin...
but the spine that held a lithe torso together
was strong the way his was not when young—

after he'd broken his own handsome, willowy neck...
The artist my new friend bestrode his studio.
Bones rattled in cupboards, the skeleton of a horse cantered off a wall.
I must say it was a *grand* studio, you could be entombed
you could be resurrected in it... We occupied mutual fragilities.

After a while we let the big Ur-cat be.
It remained unrevealed, but not, I'd say, interred.
Something else happened when he stepped into the middle of the room
to mark the spot for the next work to become.
With two hands he seemed to hold it shoulder wide.

The head of the bull would have to be *ferocious!*
And his arms, in space, circumscribed the bull as he stepped–
–balletically— towards the young women to come
leaping and dancing over the haptic head of the beast.
He mentioned *skimpy skirts* and I brought up

Leopards at banquet tables of Etruscan tombs.
Now we were, I suppose, up and running.
In Lazio, in Crete, wherever, we were in the celebratory company
of men, women and cats in the presence of bull, its weight
its burning eyes, its killing and being-killed power.

Did we dare? To speak of red and black urges, or not?
O no one likes Hemingway these days, Hemingway sucks.
He was a *dick*, yes, every good woman in a man
knows that that goes without saying.
But the animal would have to be so well *done.*

The bull itself, its grandeur, its force, would do the doing, no sweat…
Shit it was hot in that room. When it loomed, it would have to be
met with more than a *gaze:* you would have to step back
let it go past so fast it would hardly miss a horn
lost to a single knife-hand strike…And so on, I thought:

The damaged bull would have to know where to slowly turn
as if to face a mirror like the Prince in the never-ending last scene
of Visconti's film, the one where pooling shadows in the glass
reveal the aristocratic being of a man doomed by his social order
a man going under to time, a man as incredulous as he was resigned.

Minotaure vaincu, I thought, and put it out of mind.
Only to recall the etching Picasso did the very next day—
the *Minotaure mourant.* It was small consolation that
with bull so well-rendered in the middle of the room
the etching arising was *Minotaure, buveur et femmes…*

By the Shore of Swan Bay

That Beautiful Black Horse

It's too early to be fearful, or angry.
When the sun comes up it's going to feel colder.
The scum at the edge of Swan Bay will look white
but grubby, the fast water still inky.

The wind will feel like it's come across the frosty Nullaboor
but it hasn't
it's just whipped up
and fallen upon us from the Antarctic.

Lend me your beanie.

I'm carrying a candle
one of many on a kitchen tray
in the dark, step by step, a glow under my chin.

The ten thousand jam jars
(we scrounged as many as we could)
the ten thousand candle flames

and the lights are placed on the black road
for a leap of the imagination:
composing the word PEACE

at the boom gate
on the road to the secret base before dawn.

Now what?

By the paddy wagon, the horse stamps and snorts.

Unspeakable Heroes

The next year I said I didn't
want to be arrested. My
back's too frail to be man-handled.

(War can make a sissy of the best!)

I opted for the dawn peace-vigil:
candles flickering
in the eyes of horses
at the bridge to the island.

I said I didn't want
in the face of IS
to protest under the old slogans.
Our own blokes might be
sent to Mt Sinjar

to fight their way up
to show the way down
for the stranded women and children
headed for slavery.
Just the kind of war heroes we want.

Now, from my retreat
—this garden and library by the shore—
I hear that Island Security itself

stood on the hands

of my friends, stripped them
dragged them along the ground
took a hessian bag

put it over their heads
stood on their backs
said they'd get it up the arse

that they they'd kick a head
if it so much as
made a sound…

I gag on words when I think
of the rounds of war we are in
let alone try to imagine a peace.

I gag on words when I think
of the rounds of war we are in
let alone try to imagine a peace.

Photographs of My Father in Hanoi, 1972

And those who love you
will behold you
across ten thousand worlds of birth and dying.
—*Diamond Sutra,* translated by Thich Nhat Hanh

Someone has given him clip-on shades—
a touch of American General, a hint of Wilfred Burchett.
Either way, he is presence:

at meetings —leaning forward, gesticulating.
In group photographs —all in row outside some office,
with him on a top step, his short new friends smiling slightly
below him, one holding a pen like a cigarette.
Among ruins —a school or hospital, a factory with a skeletal water tower.

Bitumen gleams with oil and rain.
Everyone's white shirt is soaked
(but for the local in the black shirt, helmet on)...

And in this one he has his hands on his hips.
He was seldom like that.
His powers were self-effacing.
But here he is with a kind of triumphant grin
as if he's been fending off the B52s.

Each man with his feet the same distance apart:
like a platoon put at ease.
Crumpled trouser legs reflected in the slick.
Murky shapes beneath their feet
on their Ho Chi Minh trail, in shadow, in mud.

Proud father. Noble father, my brave old man—
although he's not old yet, I'm older than him now.
He's grown stronger by being somewhere else.

Indoors, he is attentive, placid, entirely peaceful.
You can see by the way the Vietnamese are turned towards him.
Mind you, they sit in their chairs like mice
and he is heavy in his. But there's that vase of flowers—
tall between the men meeting under the French windows.

And everyone knows (they could be lilies or irises)
everyone knows that the humid air coming in the window
to touch the men and the flowers is a movement
a conversation to welcome the hungry ghosts.

But he would not have said that.
He did not mention the airy-fairy things.
What he would have loved was the Chinese character
with the vertical and the two horizontal strokes:

Man beside Heaven and Earth—meaning Humanity.
That's what is clear, it gives the clue to his cock-a-hoop.
He left home to affirm
Humanity on the pyre of war.
'We were up at four running for the shelters, in our pyjamas.'

He knew *that* sounded thin, that it was nothing to be jaunty about!
But there's no disguising his life-death elan:
that he was there, in the burning world
that he was being 'solid' with Humanity
that he was not here, where nothing happens.

No wonder he never showed them to my mother.
No wonder he did not get to speak
of Hanh's *'Lotus in a Sea of Fire'*.
As he held on, like grim death, to Humanity.

Ambassador (Saigon 1964)

The Venerable
Thich Quang Duc
Is burning

Beside the *Ambassador*
A new one, with its bonnet up
The can of gasoline

Stranded on the bitumen…

The *Sanga* are rushing forward
Everyone has a shifty sideways look
Especially the one with the immortal
Camera Lucida…

But they could be listening
Rather than looking
Taking a leaf out of Lord Buddha's book—
The Lotus that teaches *hearing*

The *woosh* at the heart of things.

The flaming monk
Their friend and loved one
Is as straight as a dye.
The wind is at his back.

His skull and nape, as yet
Are as they were, unscathed
As a flame shoots from the forehead
Licks his lips

Sizzles at the throat.

The rest is a roar of billowing—
Straight from the heart
Out along the ground
As if to message napalm.

Some Sangha
Are agape at being
Vanquished, or clarified
Their teacher drunk on fire.

Is he flowing outwards
Or inwards and
Does it matter which?

The war rushes on.
Death will achieve nothing, nothing.
Hear Zazen-man burn, burn—

Think of him as
A hero for our times.
He is cooked meat, his after-life sleeps—

Such self-discipline!

Nor can you see his feet.
The smell of sardines
As fumes engulf them.

No time for prayer
When Dragon eats air.

Plum Juice

Without realising
I turned the page
with wet fingers
on my new copy
of Du Fu
smearing *The Sick Horse.*
Later, when I thought them dry
I came to *Facing the Snow*
the pictures he painted
crackling
with pure lament:
Above the battlefield
many new ghosts are crying;
steeped in sorrow
a lone old man is chanting.

The ladle lies useless
the wine jar toppled over;
the stove grows cold,
red embers slowly fading…

And still my touch was dark
a purply red
an indelible ink
my brush swollen
to write an end
to our running wars.
No news comes
from anywhere this winter.
In empty air
a sad old man is writing.

Murmured Conversations

Politics

You might need to take up karate again
if only to take off your own head
in the mirror of fake news

The lies are so thick on the ground.
You can hear the crunching underfoot—
slugs galore, slugs born in sophist throats.

Worse than sophists. You'll need to
wring or break—one strike—their necks:
speech has little to do with it.

They drink *Round Up.*
They munch each other's fingernails
which the best have pulled out.

They have stopped screaming
and you can't scream these days
but you went through a recent phase

or phrase, the framing of your abuse
animus, homicidal desires, new insights:
'To love thy neighbour is an act of aggression'

You know the goody two shoes teaching
on anger, revenge, blood lust; what you want
is to get your hands on their tiny minds

cruel eyes, fingers into those eyes—
an emergency strike, forget the etiquette, yes
blind them and bind them, take them out…

Ever think you would be like this?
Thank them then. They have shown you something.
They have drawn you out of the Pathos Self

Osu, Sempai. Fight freely around the empty bowl
bow and strike, strike and bow. Go at it again
Be the vital young clown you thought you were

Work your way around the floor
As the nightmare roars, revive right ceremony
Perform the Fire Ode, abandon funeral rites

Sutra

What's happened to those *murmured conversations?*
The gentle links between verses, words, whispers?

All that might happen under a lowly thatched roof
after the ten thousand thoughts pass through

in a single night, and which the morning
brings the light into, gently gently lifting shadows

as heart-mind departs from moth-wings
assembles in units of a poem to be woven

together by men attuned to each other, their buds
and stems of poems, and to the spirit of enlightenment.

How could you have travelled so far into darkness?
Some poems, gleefully thrummed, expel illumination.

They are acts of war. They dwell in vanity
can shame you to death, banish you to Bardo—

one false note and you have no poem of worth
or to speak of, you have kinky murders at midnight.

I think (is this the link?) (I dimly realise now)
A poem mangled in wilful conception

gives the game away: it reveals a desire
to be priest above all else, some vain character in black

a spirit failing in himself, in health, faith in service:
someone cruel to dogs, a beast of a man who kicks

living things out of his way, who thinks
nothing of treading on a harmless cockroach...

In the time of poet-monk Shinkei
the character for dog was written

on the new-born's brow as a charm
to protect the child from evil.

Your poem had no feeling for dog or cockroach
so in love with itself is your word-spirit.

You remain fond of the poem even as you feel its evil.
Who knows what *minima moralia* will fire you next?

All you knew while writing
was that one dark link would lead to the next...

Now try to find your way back...
Wordlessly if need be, no eye, no ear, no tongue...

Greg Dening's Beloved Beach Crossings

He seemed to have swum in
from a long way out
from an island we dimly knew
but which he had loved so well
to bring us the news direct:

that to be walked safely ashore
you need a torso tattooed:
that you have to have signed on
with women of the hearth
picked a ripe daughter for the full moon
pinned her freely to the earth.

Imagine he showed you his tongue—
the cross drawn in black ink
an organ bedded between
short white teeth and lips carved in coconut.
Hungry ghost of the Pacific that he was.

His song a melody of relativities—
drums under the palms
a jig to the trade winds
a hymn to the fruits of autumn.
His true god Negative Capability
surfing in fleets of catamarans.

You felt you could sail with him
anywhere, meet anyone you wanted
or dreamt of. He had what some call
a free mind, an intelligence
proud of its spinnaker. His dictim:
Know your own heart, and hull.

Then you'd catch sight of him
far out and alone in a long-boat
his oars at dainty rest
the prow piled high with skulls.
As if the sight of death becalmed him.

Such fine details we'd never tire of reading
from his beautiful and terrible archive
that I came to feel before he died
the sublime service to give him
might be hard-put for ritual.

Immortals and the Heather

For Gerry Simpson

A London friend writes to me he's planning
to take his mother to the Highlands.
I remember my own mother
among the granite and kangaroo grass of the You Yangs.

His mother, with whom he dances in his kilt
is still going strong, bless her brave heart.
She must be the kind of woman who knows
what Hugh MacDiarmid called *The Whole Keyboard.*

Not unlike my venerable mother-in-law
who has as much music in her as a mouse in a haystack:
she is simply all enduring. I have named her *Immortal.*
And she smiles as if she is full of sappy thistle.

Once I thought my mother was firm of foot
and as steady as she was devoted to me
her only child. But, among the boulders that day
she heaved and sagged to the hard ground.

My father reached her first, me second
the magpies after that, as she lay there ashen.
In *The Ballad of Narayama* the son carries
his mother on his back to the top of the mountain.

My mother did not then 'pass' (as the feeble in speech say).
She just hung on, as mothers can, until we carry them no more.
Or until we bow to them who would yet hold us—
amorous sons of fortune in laps of recent luxury.

Love Child Blues

Today, I almost ran over my first wife.

She was near the curb, her hair falling silver
grey & straight when she leaned over
to a dog as hairy as her dusky, blue mohair coat
hem touching the hockey-fit calves
I knew so well.

Slightly bending her legs, saving her back
that lumber region, scooping the dog into her arms
cradling it against her breasts
stepping out like an Apostle
supple as she crossed the road.

I nearly went by before seeing her.
I'm sure she didn't see me:
old rat kept going.
Her cornflower eyes I held in my mind
until well out onto the highway.

Ten years of our youth we poured
into clear blue pools
& she stood half-undressed
before the wardrobe the night I came clean.
Naked in her cry: why why why.

A rat would have lied
& I didn't.
And (years later): Don't you wish we'd had a *love* child?
Way back, I had tried to explain:
I was not yet man enough.

Shostakovich on the tape deck:
his furious strings stretching
across the snowy Steppe.
Always the highway.
She was as fair as Lara then.

The Last European

How is it I am still alive? I'll tell you I'm alive because there's a temporary shortage of death. This is said with a grin, which is on the far side of a longing for normalcy, for an ordinary life.
—John Berger, 'Undefeated Despair'

I've been soliciting
a commission to visit John Berger—
the better, perhaps, to write about him.

A flight to Geneva, a bus ride
and I'd be there
in his village with a view of Mt. Blanc.

But why even dream of disturbing
the peace of a man at 90
when I can write about him here?

I realized this a minute ago
as I was handling
a pound of fresh butter.

It firmly exists
as Berger's honouring of Mahmoud
Darwish exists—

along with Berger's drawings
each spindly line intense
etched in sorrow.

I think of him as the last Englishman
to be European. He knew when to leave
London, posh galleries be damned.

He valued scythes in alpine village sheds
where snowfalls upheld
the vast blues of history.

That motor bike took him
no further east than Istanbul:
about all the Orient you get in Berger

is 'Tokyo Street' in Ramallah
where Dawsish has his grave.
The Middle East was as far as he went.

Walls and prayers, rubble and resistance—
arising from his 'undefeated despair.'
It's fair to say he'd understand

this staying at home with a writing brush
covering rice paper with Chinese characters—
'integrity', 'humanity', 'vital spirit', and so on.

I must work with his hopeful breath—
strokes subtle and strong, their alignments
whole-hearted with all of my body.

New Alice Springs Poems

Right Love

Who has written
with right love
about this hard light?

It flicks pebbles, sharpens
reeds, makes ghost gums
amorous for dance.

In Hidden Valley—
atomic clarity of dusk.
They stand around
not looking
as we drive up.
Kids with little salt lakes
glinting on their upper lips.

We are there to help.
We will take your rubbish.
Just bring
as the sun sinks
the bag of rattling cans
that *sound* like the light.

In Hidden Valley
I got caught in the glare
the amplifying net it cast
each of us with pores open
glances shooting past
the whole camp under daytime stars.

Then, back on the bitumen
the night time slump
the light no longer peeling
off you, or them
the conversation about them
starting all over again.

No Maggots Today

She had gales in her
bosom and belly
a sashay rolled
into a clap of mirth

an almost mocking
laughter up on the range
as if she left the bloke
in the ute for dead.

It was a great wind-up
outside Yeperenye—
as if to say
Life's a joyous thing

with no maggots
in the middle.
Just wish I'd seen
her happy thunder face.

She had a loose
denim skirt, a dimpled
lumbar region—
buttocks that talked.

A man standing there
could but carry
his heart
strung around his neck.

Witchetty Tree

Falling away like that
dramatically out
from the trunk's base
a spray for each dead branch
a switch like a witch's broomstick
waiting to be lit.

Missionary Kempe, brittle jawed
had the slit gaze of God's eyes
a trying not to appear
suspicious look
at the short-lived trunk
with its rotten root.

The grubs are the thing.
Nutty when roasted.
Spasms like your gut
if it was cut open:
from nape to sweet bowel
becomes the whole feast.

Everywhere here
I walk around with my face
in earth and in fire.
The crystal starlight lacerates.
Yesterday's sunset
seen through the scrub
was a lovely pale lime.

Hymn

It is a light, which the wind blew out.
—Georg Trakl

My friend who has befriended them
Has some good news, good news.

We feel it to be wholly true.
We dwell in the name's sweet light.

Arretyaletyale
arDah chala-chala is what they say.

Newborn boy for the Hayes'—
Native Title Owners
at the White Gate Camp.

Baby Warren—Honeyeater
arDah chala-chala.

O may the wind be kind to him.
May the wind be kind to him.

Medicine Stories, Drawing Circles

1

This will do me—
looking like Uta Uta Tjangala.
A warrior with a red
band around his skull.

A warrior with a wife
in a wheel barrow
(later a wheel chair).
Proper married man, that one.

Uta Uta's *Old Man's Story* has
two one legged men
resting at their camp:
body paint and bush tucker to hand.
Patterns and fires all night long.

He was painting and dancing
drinking and whispering
long as long. Old man
with never-ending view.

2

The other day I got shaved
cut open and stitched up.
I think, the knife-man said
you are a bit of a sook.

He fancied himself
from a special tribe.
But, I said, I'm a smart sook
(or a lucky sook by a soak!)

whereas you, young fella
          are a bit of a boofhead
                    and a boofhead is a boofhead.
                    Healing men together after that.

See this one, I said
pointing to Uta Uta's *Medicine Story:*
          a big yam of an amorous man.
                    Sitting-down places all along
                              like waterholes, or testicles
                                        swollen and loose.
The painting's called
          Testicles Going Walkabout.
                    Fair dinkum.
After slow mending
          I had tell boofhead:
                    you must have left
                    some barbed wire
                              in my flaming groin.

3

By 80 I'm gunna be
          without pain.
          Like Paddy Bedford—
                    age to start painting again.

I remember my own old times:
          the turps running
                    like tears for my mother.

I was a boy then. Uninitiated!
          For my dad I painted the flame
                    out on the plains
                              of the refinery.

Have a funny feeling now.
          Finished with Petro Dreaming.
                    Might go back up—
                              sit on the ground.

4

Not Paddy of those sickly
          Philip Guston pinks.
                    Paddy with the ghost of his wife in his swag

or my ghost in the swag
          of my own Misses
                    dreaming among succulents
                              near waterholes:

married man and his wife
          traveling with Honey Ant Story
                    on the mend, nothing fucked up.

5

Drawing circles—
          means everything.

A Few Cheap Poems

Para-medic

Mum might have said
you can't have all those fucks
in what could be your last book.

I was ten when, unknowing
I told her to get stuffed.
The old man came running.

Look at me now.
Vivid speech for anyone who'll listen
working a siren into each line.

Hardly Touched

Calloused were her hands
from kitchen and garden.
Evening *Nivea* insufficient

The simple truth:
her tender heart was pliant
her touch not up to it.

Whereas the old man
who was good at pats
wore heavy gloves as welder and blacksmith.

Self Protection

By my second divorce
our son had a little hunch
to keep the hugs out.

His sister was all too willing
to cling to you whether
coming or going.

Quietly, each parent
waited in their own way
for one of the twelve steps.

Utopia

Not euthanasia
dished out along the wards.
Not the last gasps

but maybe the full holdings
breaths in and out—
life-shuttles

given as gifts
one to the other
with returns

the unborn
with the unborn—
cradlings.

2

Bunyah Is Beach
For Les Murray

Dear Les, I Like Your Bunyah

But my salty coast is better on hot days.
All the salt's in one place, the wet one, for one thing
and, while I seldom mistake lyrebirds
for leaf-litter, I see the gannets' diving
as authentic as the sea, ripples persistent
as your drought, which I feel for you

it's true, but I mostly think I can
barely imagine your Bunyah, Les.
I have the same but different flirtation
with the Rip, its tidal clash and depth;
the wrecks are hidden, submarine
timber stressed and bolt-rusted but

sunken ships are not like old sheds.
You have to drown or scuba dive to get rewards
for nostalgia well-earned, the timber silvered.
It's cool work, at least, also unpaid or
barely paid, that we have in common, Les.
Our iron beds were close to thin walls.

And I like the way you jet-ski words
cross-country in tracks of talk-song, ballads
skirting graveyards, bubbling recognitions.
It's your way into marine coolness of mind
as when I plunge from a high-curling wave
to be beached all in good in time, hey Les, hey.

Bunyah is beach we share, dare I say this now, Les.
Look at slopes of country below dams.
They once were dunes between boulders—
middens all round, like ancestors. Your poems
so full of mealy shell-grit, lingo shit-stripped;
words rolling and roiling on the tongue

for all their worth, as if ocean powered them.
Inland, Les, I can see where waves might dump me.
There's frog joy to a splayed joint arrival like that.
The inland I can see from a roller's crest
with its thunder and hissing sounds
that's nothing like a State Bank crash.

The Moon Man we have in common but.
His brilliance is in our blood.

Grovedale

For Beverley Farmer

Just like the wind that rebuffs you,
the snow is packed around your word
—Paul Celan

Her Favourite Munch

She tells you again, as you arrive once more, that she is dead
already: she died yesterday or the day before. Or both.

You used to say: I think I know the feeling
(after a birthday, sleeping pills, a drunken night…).

Glib. Pull your head in.
Now you say: I just wish I could bury you.

There. Knee to knee, let that sink in.
Bury you was the kindest thing you could think to say.

You did not have to think. You just said it.
Thoughtfully, she heard it, as would a crow in her fig tree.

There are scraps of food on her lovely upper lip.
The other day you clipped her fingernails.

Gothic, and as greasy as the seat of her walking frame…
You wondered about her toes, zipped up in pink.

Like dyed dead rabbits. But you are not
her keeper, you never married her, let the nurses smirk.

Anyway, she intends (an odd word) a cremation.
In the absence of a sky burial, you could set her alight.

Remember the friend who said she was a pure flame?
The walker's so filthy it would go up in a tic…

Dusk. And she's still in her pyjamas. This morning
she declared a holiday. No one need touch her today.

Huge, cobalt blue, Matisse flowers on silently
screaming snow white. She might even be enjoying

the look of that look. You could turn up in a dressing gown
—stand the other side of the bed, just like her favourite Munch.

Time Out of Mind

She'd been counting children again.

The dead ones the nurses swaddle each day
to smuggle out in wheelie bins.

She has no hair, she's in despair
her son's not there, he's overseas indefinitely.

He sold the house beneath her. The nurses
rake it in. Behind their mitts she sees them grin.

Eventually, gently, you take your leave:
abandon the bad air of the one hundred beds

a gust of which you met on going in
like garbage at the sliding doors

or a whiff of rotten teeth.
Then, the building exhaled, and you managed

to step outside to breathe the ten thousand things
glinting in a winter noon. Amazing.

The world awaiting: the empty paddock of the dairy
the place where, last time you were there

a young black bull glowered among its bevy.
You held each other's vital gaze.

In another paddock: burnt trees, dead wood
un-cut green grass, platoons of wattle birds

and the frisky, plump post-coital rabbits
playing about with time on their side.

A vista of eternal noon, and
further across, on the blue horizon—

the outcrop of the Yawangs, like grinding stones
rising from the lava plain:

Wathaurung time, a Dreaming
with never-ending space between daylight stars.

Waves of feeling rather than seeing.
It was a *base line*

a kind of melodic downbeat
The New Yorker's music critic spoke of

as you drove in—regarding Purcell
and the stream delivered by Dylan.

You told her about this. She seemed to know.
She remembered how you love the radio.

Lost Contact Lens

What is the prayer
when there is here?

Take my hand…

Give me your proper name.
Yes, it's a gamble.

Nothing to write home about.
A gift-horse in the mouth.

A dark matter.
It's what you think it is

when thinking is a bid
for the way, when that's not clear

even when to hand.
The name that confounds

is no name
is ashes of the mind

is the evening on waking
is that blind in the morning.

Little Remorse

The coming words in the heart
that was between us…

So patient we are in the ward
the visitor and the one
being visited.

Knees sometimes touching
knees between, your tiny steps
slippers wanting flight, but no—
the wheeler would get away.

Our unstuck silence—
like former speech returning…

The milky Nescafe is luke-warm
in its mid-blue cup.
Soon it will be cold
but not as cold as snow.

Words cease
to be hard-packed—
this patience we have
for whatever is slowly coming forth.

Give it time.
A minute ago a nurse spotted us smiling.
She almost stepped back
to look again
at strangers in a snow-storm.

We were just remembering
those literary prize-givings—
the pomp & praise
of self-punishing years.

Days when no heart-word came forth
until dawn, if at all…
Your night murmurs.

Days when I should have washed
my mouth *out*—

Byzantine Telephone

When it rings it could be him, her son—
a father adrift in Hamburg, clinging to his wife

and child, granny's raison d'être
who now might have a German name.

It's all there, this galloping loss, in the voice
she doubts is him. It's a trick

as her own mothering was a trick, a delusion of being
able to love, to have, to hold and name.

He has two names and both are absent
neither the Greek or the English one entirely

him: nor will either return in time, will be seen again
or heard before she dies, that's for sure, that's as certain

as the trouble she has with the smart phone
it's stupidity is a sin. His father said, *give him up*

or he'll be on a steamer to Thessolonica.
His father, a would-be Trojan, strutted heroism.

She handed him over, faked surrender, stitched up
a peace and that man could not be him

ringing now, or before. Her punishment called.
The nurses say he's just returned

but they're pulling strings behind the screen.
It's like a sunblind, she knows a sunblind

when she sees one. You yourself gave her a date
for his return, but who's to say that's the case?

Now she wants the window open, the slot that slides
near the floor, with a mesh to keep the spiders out:

a good thing. The breeze cools
the heels when it's not freezing toes.

Dear Midnight

hear deep in
with your mouth
—Paul Celan, *The Trumpet Place*

Did she call for her end?
Or not?
Another knot of not again?

You'd touched her hand.
She had brushed your knee
said sorry and murmured
something of an unknown order...

A nurse popped in.
She called her Dear.
Did you need...?
No thanks— return fire
dropping the name
of the nurse on the floor.

Our tête-à-tête again:
words lie back on her tongue
between the dentures
and scummy lips.

One day, I said, offering a tissue
for her mouth:
you can wipe it here.
And she dabbed about.

She did not speak
as I made to... *converse.*
So that she could with trembling hand
water her silences.
Outside, marigolds in shelves of seedling trays.

Sweet basil too high for the rabbits.

I could see the sapling girl in her.
The thin shy one with a watering can
trickling drops on delphiniums.
(Iphigenia was yet to come…)

I want to die is
what I thought she'd said.
Like Virginia, yes.
Maybe Sylvia, God I hoped not.

All right, I will take you.
All right I have no right
but you only have to ask.
I'll meet you on the pier at midnight.

Your pier, we all have our piers.
At midnight, yes, if you want—
with the tide wine-dark and racing out.
The pockets filled heavily and the blood thundering.

I imagined going into the sea with her.
The better for her to launch herself truly—
if she was game, game
her pockets loaded with stones, stones…

Most love is wasted, she once told me…

And here comes another nurse
who does not knock, the pet
a lass with a nice time-piece.
She does not know which of us, if anyone, spoke.

Another one to forget our names
who thinks I am my friend's husband
who believes we are deaf.
Dear, the kindly ones shout, *Dear.*

We are laying plans to cut their throats.

Honestly—

there's no expression
in your face

or very little to the clay
it has become
in recent years.

It is perhaps the mask
you long desired.
It cannot signal hey

hello or what do you
want, why didn't you
ring first, come back again

some other
time? One day soon
if you want, I'll ring

you. You said those
things over a full
election cycle.

One day I returned
to your change
of government—

a bunker of necessity.
By then I wore my own mask
with a wounded heart.

My task: to imagine
your funeral the way
you'd long been

imagining
without my noticing.
You faded with barely

a name for it.
And now, thank you so much
(a sickening phrase)

for letting me break
your face open
the day I read

the first review
of your last book
to you.

Your smile showed forth
like the shaft
of light

fallen
or delivered
into the room.

I felt it strike
the back of my neck
as a voice said

This is
the happiest day
of my life.

Accolades.
Blooming of their own accord!

On the last visit
your were so ill-kempt
I could only put my face
my cheek-bones between
your shoulder blades…

That was the other
fine farewell.

Commotions
For Fay Zwicky

Mister Lincoln or Camp David

Cormorants at dusk fly in
under the life-boat shed at the pier's end.
Each arrives at their end
of a day's fishing, their beaks
suddenly open, panicky, necks back
as they gain timber and shadow.

For a second I think
they are choking on air
that they might not get to
folding their wings peacefully for the night
that they might need more medication.
Or somesuch.

Ringing off, I can still hear your voice.
I keep wanting to ring you back.
Who knows what we might have chosen
to talk about: the Self and its vicissitudes
I suppose, the poems that confined us
the Crazy Janes that would not.

In this garden, there's a dark red rose
on a tall straight stem. A blunt man would
just pick it for his friend: and how we cursed
our blights of bluntness. Some of its petals
are edged with black, from frostbite.
I can tell you now it's either called

Mister Lincoln or Camp David.
But you would know that.
The Camp David is thorny.
Each day, when I take my pick of whatever
I can hear your throaty voice
the old smoke still roiling in it.

At Last Your Book

has arrived.

Your picture on the cover.
Glamorous, you said drolly
almost self-reproachfully.

It is painful to have known such beauty.
How do we live up to such a thing—
the feathers within so constantly ruffled:

chronically so, like coughing
like notes pouring the wrong way
out of a flawed self, you

you with your bosom wholly
covered with gentians. (I'll put the book
beside Lawrence's *Last Poems*.)

I'm not even sure it matters
that we hardly met or were
when we did, like telegraph poles

marching down opposite sides of the street.
Once, in a poem about my son
I used the word 'commotion'.

Over the phone I heard you murmur approval.
That will do. We were poetically
attuned to each other's commotions.

Failing Better

Another thing we had in common.
A suspicion of ideas. Yes, really.

Oh, we had a certain facility for them—
as Flaubert had a certain regard for Bouvard.

We could dance with them as in
quick step, barn dance, jive, dive

into the pools of them post-war
post-peace, post-theory, etc.

(As we alluded to Etc over the phone
we could hear the butcher birds

leaving our gardens in dismay
when all we sought was a parrot

captivated by the *Simple Heart.*)
Start again.

We knew how to listen into
Each other, inhaling the secret spaces

taking liberties, extending sympathy
with flounderings, failures of authenticity

the clod-hopping muck-ups
of love's diction, of utterances that sought

to play cello for Elgar, a shakahatchi
for Basho, colours for Matisse...

Hear words failing me again.
I have been sleepless again, I ring you again

to find you three hours behind but awake
already, having watered your garden already.

Already already already.
I joined you in Jewish ways of knowing.

You boasted that you were a Buddhist already!
More laughing.

Pipes

Then there was the call
when we thought about happiness.

But did not name it.
Back then you'd had the piano.

I swam and painted
the petrochemical complex.

We grew up into
our performances and offerings.

One day, we mentioned evil.
Iago, you said.

One day, marriage was mentioned, as an if.
And what if I had not said yes?

you said with a yes laugh.
That will be in the obit, I said.

Words are treacherous.
We agreed on that.

I was not even serious
I love my present wife.

You probably drive her mad, you said.
No, I fucking don't.

There was another day
when we plunged, almost, into confessions.

Bordello experiences of various kinds.
'Bordello experiences' interpreted widely.

The shame of shame when it is true experience.
We put that in our pipes.

White Light

'Camp David' is in bloom.
You get a whiff of it before
arriving at its feet, its face:

it's on the north wall of the studio
in full sun, making steam
out of morning humidity
that will bake the afternoon.

The crimson is to die for.
Crimson is how too many
are dying. What would you think of—

Ramallah or Tel Aviv?
Jerusalem, I suppose…
Places where you'd pray
without your god.

But that's not quite you either.
'I'm a Buddhist, too!'
I once was startled
to hear you claim.

Together, I'd say,
we could try too hard.
We jockeyed to ride on 'Universal'
before it could be scratched.

Why, only the other day
my wife sat down with a Psychic
only to be told that her husband

was gambling with the spirit
of a venerable woman
a dark beauty

who was still hanging around—
a guardian, of sorts, some kind of writer
a poet perhaps, a performer—

Don't forget I was a performer!
The Psychic must have heard you say
as you said it to me.

Back here, by the sea
your photograph still looked up
from the couch, absorbing light
like a cuttlefish on hot sand.

Just recently, I've moved
your poems to a shelf
where it was propped up
as if waiting to bud…

It's going to take me
ages to know
what to rest each side of it
what noble company it will keep.

Arms Full of Flowers

For Patricia O'Donnell

Mainly Chekhov

Among the images as yet surviving her
my friend has—'with the monotonous hollow
sound of the sea rising up from below'
speaking of peace, and 'of the eternal sleep
awaiting us'—three beloved images:

her great grandfather, as a boy, painted by Titian.
But no, it could not be, he lived at the time of Mazzini
he has that man's lustre at the *Risorgimento:*
the budding manhood is in the lips and vital nostrils
he is going to grow up and be—
well, anything he wants to be, in effect.

And there, on the wall, in a recess between shelves
a young woman is competing with pastel carnations;
she is misted by them, as if the paint has faded
but no, no, again, my dear friend's mother was painted
tonally in a soft blur of natural beauty
that was beyond her, like a Giorgione.

From Milano, city of secrets and private lives.
City guarded by the lake of paradise, which Pound loved;
city with a view of snowy peaks and death
that-cannot-be-denied peaks, which Lawrence loved.
The gods feast up there, luxuriate below
saunter in the beautiful arcades in comfort and liberty.

Autonomously, self-governingly and subtly
visible is the other portrait she loves.
At first glance he is in shadow.
You can just make him out through the lattice
of the bookshelf, his white dress-shirt and dark jacket
his summer hat reminiscent of *Death in Venice*—

except that, when the shelf is rolled back
Chekhov reveals himself with pince-nez, fob-watch
and a beard as trimmed as you would expect
of a small, retiring, stunningly observant man
forever noting the habits of cockroaches, sparrows
'and the higher aims of our existence'.

It is almost too good to see my old friend again.
We barely need to talk. She wants to speak of me.
But I know it is a ruse. She likes the roses I cannily brought.
She eats the cake, she defers, without saying
to the knowing, scientific mode of Chekhov at Oreanda
near Yalta, and his unforgettable story, *The Lady with the Dog.*

And I must borrow the book! I have to take it
home to see if I have it already. Of course, she surrenders
the book, she is a genius at knowing another's needs,
and later, shamelessly, I comb my shelf
to see that I *do* have one, and will not need to cling
surreptitiously cling, to this thing of hers at all.

Besides, I see that it was me who has inscribed
the second copy I now have in my hands!
A gift of twenty years ago, when we were middle-aged
and lived by the sea sometimes believing
in 'unceasing progress towards perfection.'
Another Chekhovian detail…

Before dawn, I woke by a shore where the wind had died.
I imagined her immortal
and the good doctor's shudder at the pill I swallow.

Poppy

I didn't get to the dens in Penang when I thought of them.
And I was not so thinking, necessarily, this morning when
I looked down into the face of the full flower
that thick showgirl pink, its green within
lime or a light jade, petals in clitoral bloom.

I bowed imagining the cats watching or the crow
that was in the branch above me yesterday
its cloak folded, sheaved, waiting for me to return
inside, inside is what I sought, I suppose, O Lord
give me more inside, inside what a full poppy is about.

As it is, mind is as good as full of fatality these days.
Suicide in one form or the other, and, speaking of
self-arming/harming, being disarmed or surrendering arms—
all those far-fetched things on exploding frontiers
across fields and fields under never-ending Inanna moons…

Still, I have decided to bring a single poppy inside
for the Buddha. It will make a good show, it will
be a reminder of one damn thing after another.
Back then, I didn't believe ole Jaw Bone Snyder
when he was so casual about Bamiyah.

Remember when bodies fell from towers
like birds like stones like stones in pairs
ole married couples going down past
the unbroken windows. Who would have thought?
Pick a flower for the non-thought the pre-thought:

this morning, pretending I was never born
that I am unborn, barely in need of a coffin
for the funeral I must go to, all I need is armfuls
of flowers she had in the foyer of her hotel—
so many then, I did not know their names.

Badly Mothered, Blazing Chaos

For Sam Hamill

When the Third Patriach of Zen, Sengstan, was still a student…
he went to his Master and said, 'I am diseased; please cleanse me of my sin.'
The Master said, 'Bring me your sin and I will cleanse you of it.'
Sengstan thought a long time. 'I cannot get at it.'
'Then I have cleansed you of it.'
—Sam Hamill, 'Sitting Zen, Working Zen, Feminist Zen'

Your rugged smile, Sam.
It had been around O
it had been around.
You had Utah grit between your teeth.

Worn down at fifteen
you cleared off to Haight Ashbury
where you got yourself two 'little habits'—
a fist-full of poetry here, a load of smack there…

Then, half a century later, you land here!
To sup at a safe antipodean table
like some new artificial paradise—
with us 'being kind' (as you said of me and my wife)

to our post-op guest:
a man weakened but still chewing
the fat of poetry and politics and socialism.
You were the first Yank I'd heard say 'socialism'.

Seemed we'd both arrived at a good place.

I asked you, apropos the youthful street life
the muggings, the jail terms
if you were 'still an arsehole'.
Your grin could have filled a flagon.

Today, you would have been 75
just weeks before me, another month
breaking onto another beach of poetry:

black wave after black wave of blank verse
Zen ruminations and whatnot—
little tsunamis of hope, literary effects
and paraphrase, Classical homage, subservience
to truculent beauty in our own idiom.

All the while casting a cold eye on the college kids—
their fathers, the bankers and industrialists
the arms-manufacturers, the gun-keepers
and the gatekeepers. The anti-socialist cunts…

But we loved women, we really did.
Good women were what we needed
good cunt or no good cunt (we're drunk again!).
Fellow cunt-worshipers, not mother-fuckers.

Anything but harm a mother, and that's the truth.

The mothers who harmed us came on this earth
to teach us some truth, that's the truth too.
They taught us to treat all things as equal.
They led us into all manner of translation.

Remember when I asked you why
Basho left that kid by the side of the road?
The cruelty of haiku! More had to be said!
I was uncomprehending, incredulous: you far less so.

We get what we get the way a good line
finds its full-stop. Only to start over again
as pipings on pipings became our life—
Taoists while hardly knowing and

trying to resist the disconsolate
making this line better than that
(or at least as good as that jerk's). Anyway
a strong line does not permit a man to put himself down…

When we left the table I held up some Chinese.
'Aw', you drawled, 'I'm not working on that right now.'
Wish I'd had a line from your Chuang Tzu:
The blazing chaos is the light that guides the sage.

And to think: back then, the authorities thought
they were giving you a clear choice:
'Do real time, Hamill, or join the Marines'.

And that cleaner of latrines in Okinawa
the old man who showed you the interiors
of temples… When did it hit you that
secret teachings include powers to set up type?

Behind me the candle burns, Sam.

3

The Gusts

For Meredith McKinney

A translator of Basho wrote to me:
that the poem is not in the words.
The poem lies in the hum behind the words.

Listen to it now—
Or see it now, in this case here:
The poem is between lines, or behind the lines

as if it is lying in wait, readying itself for combat:
words versus silence, words barely holding
the trench from collapsing but

already I have defeated the poem.
Made an ordeal of it. Made it mud
or blood splattered…

All my life I have had a whistle in my throat.
To improve the breath I learnt to swim
from shore to pier, from pier to shore.

Various wives have seen me swim far out—
waving to them as I dive for poems
treading water as if to die for a poem.

Then, through long blue days
when the wind is hot and offshore
I can see, hearingly, gusts of poems in the dunes.

Chuang Tzu and a Bad Back in Seoul

The true men of old
Slept without dreams…
True men breathe from their heels

1
Days grounded here.
I try to walk and a blade
slices around a disc.

Like Ting the Cook
whose knife work
has gone wrong.

The Tao a long way off.
My wife also—
a Hemisphere away.

She knows my plight
I'll Skype her later
from this buzzy Writer's Centre

which has, bless them
a screen-print of me
all over the kitchen window.

I must stay on. I must get up
read more poems, earn my keep.
She gets it, she's got gigs herself

and won't be home
if I return; she'll be
in a rainforest somewhere

unmedicated and clear
pain-free, singing with
that voice of 'Absolute Roaming'—

'Making All Things Equal'
in a cosmos of notes
unfurling in her hair.

2

'My body is chaos
my mind in order'.
Hope I have

with the recurring picture
of Ting the Cook
dismembering that ox.

The material body—its gore
and the empty space
for the blade.

Nothing uttered, the blade un-blunted
everything falling off
the bone as it ought.

The ox was young
and old in the instant—
ever-ready in life

beautifully handled
in death. Rightly touched
and cut, pain-free.

O I like a good knife in my hand.
That my body be as balanced!
That a juicy moon fall into my lap!

Confined to barracks I am, but
neither this hip or my cracked laughter
has brought me down.

3

This doing nothing can be
in the flow of the present—

not to mention the pallid
capsule of a morphine derivative.

Even so, the Tao is as real
as my breath, a cup of water, shit—

even shits like the old
dictator next door

his massacres behind him.
His dogs bark all night.

I use the term easily
(Tao, I mean, not shit)

but shit has to be included
without any reference

to the numbers he killed.
Master Chuang knew that

without making too much of it.
OK then, this Taoist shit

is suddenly making total sense!
Don't help me up.

Leave me be on the slippery floor
I'll stay stretched out

in sympathy, dreaming democracy
among dead poets

and the late-coming poets
who arrive drunk, empty-handed

having forgotten my pizza.
Planet earth gives off its emissions.

Leave me be in the night
breeze among the old pines.

4

Lychee horizon at dawn—a kind of hum.
Egg-shell blues in the tiles at dusk.

These lovely stone pines
stepping in and out of shadow.

Today, what move will not
re-twist the knife?

Pain is the Tao's moon.
And the dogs have gone quiet.

If I Skype her now she'll hear me
getting ahead of myself. *Listen!—*

have you not heard
the rush of tones?

Dusk

I climbed up here
to take stock of the glorious dusk—
measure it in some way
a 'poetic' way, some say
smiling as if they know what's left.

I see crimson
apricot, the pale aqua, all that
in sky, bay and sand bank —
effortlessly transforming
as we like to think of ourselves

doing before it's
too late.
But ever so quickly a heavy sky
is empty of birds. Just gone.
As if sketched in charcoal on slate
greasy crayon on black marble.

In odd spots, out over the water
swans graze on toxic sea grass.
And nothing seems right
with this bat flitting
this way and that, furious

seeming to soar, supersonically
only to drop sideways
in spasms, then darting straight
but off its track again—
nervous disorder being

its way, its way, its way.
Then when I shut my eyes
    to join the poor thing in blindness
    envious of its cave
        all it did was disappear.

Birthday

No other like this one.

The world so dewy.

Roses and snapdragons climbing the air
out of a vase on the lazy susan

a blooming purple storm
like that rare thing, a virtuous bishop!

And to sit with it, first up
on your birthday morning

along with the black cat
the dark soul of Cat, the immortal one

from a Pharaoh's tomb.
But all that was nothing

compared to the shot glass
waiting on the table of the top deck.

Overnight it had half filled
with rain, glistening with crystal winter.

So, having drunk from it this morning
the miracle is you can fill it once more

this moonrise evening.
Her face, also, still adorable.

I've Had You in Mind, Mista Crow

What do you know?
Strutting a fine line
on bone-dry strips of kelp

as brittle, as black, as your prime self.

As I've been thinking of you
there's crow in me as too
believe it or not Mista Crow…

What are you doing
so close to the ocean with its
heavy swells from the south?

Anyway, here's a little secret.

I'd prefer to be a gull.
I would like to be a putrid white—
own up to my load of virus'.

You with your affinity to rats.
Me with my penchant for lice.
What a pair we make

by the wintering shore
and the spring-lulls
with new schools of squid coming in

lured to lights on the pier
where they are hauled up
for their timely deaths, Mista Crow

squirting their ink onto planks
where any old bird can read
the calligraphy of final things…

Here's something
you might not know, Mista Crow.
There are peace-talks again.

Don't ask me where, exactly.
But they are persisting
in having them.

The war-dead stir
in their new coffins.
All they lack is another PM

to prop them up
in mendacious light—
give them a new view of the sites

of victories bound to be
defeats by god knows what.
Mista Crow, you're a hero on that kelp.

Imagine the coming peace, Mista Crow.
Imagine the lively white I'll be by then.
All sheen, no end to me

Restless Under Full Moon

Listen!—it's never ending analysis that wounds us.
—T'ao Chi'ien

Later in life he had a thing about black
he could not shake off.

It was not a hole
not even dark energy
so much as a negative gleam
here and there on the body
with its leaden heart.

Image-wise, he could not place it
or quite put a finger on it.
The high, light points were on forehead
cheek, hip and shoulder—
the eye lands, wasp-like
making itself diaphanous near collar bone.

Inside the fist he could see black
& under his tongue, a fair way back
past the mysterious *leukoplakia*.
Some days, between his teeth looked black.
The thought of words
felt like a biopsy, or surgery.

There can be a sheen to black:
think Bernini, Donatello (anyone but Michelangelo).
The black at issue is also sticky. Like peat.
Thinking adheres to the stuff…

Black dreaming, black heels, black beauty
black love. How often did she say O
you have such dark thoughts.

He had to grin when
he defended himself as a Realist.
He felt her recoil. Everything is beyond matter.

You'll tire yourself out, she said.

No! He hated wearing *her* out
even under the reign
of daylight savings.
See—he could not resist saying
night gets stolen from us.

Pearl and Tides

'But the world is muddy witted and does not
understand me', wrote Yu Quan, not me.

Poor filthy gulls, a plague on each wing—
each feather a study in anti-anti-biotics:

immortal seethings of life
each little thing with its wheeze box.

'Round my neck moon bright jewels
and a precious jade in my girdle'...

Then comes the 'but' about muddy wit
and the crossing of un-named rivers.

'I climbed up Kun-lun and ate the flower of jade.'
Tell me another one, Yu Quan...

Yet I read on, soaring with *Songs of the South*
& wanting to shave my head—

'For my days are sure to end in dark confusion.'
& wanting to laugh like Janice Joplin—

Shaman lady with that pure load
of snowy powder after the last song—

too good by half, too good by half:
dragon singing waves and the clouds.

Shit Buddhist

1

For ages I've known myself
to be a shit Buddhist.
Proof is—I want to be
buried in the earth.

I don't want to go up in flames—
And come down
in flecks of ash
for scattering on air or water.

And I want my beloved
to be buried with me
side by side
for eternity

or until we are bones
bones that once were
bones travelling underground
ancestors can stand on.

I have a spot in mind
from where you can see
the lighthouse and hear
the rollers over the reef.

The need for this
is deeper than I can say.
Unholy is my desperation
to drown in earth with her.

2

I saw her wince.
Prior to uttering my request
I asked her to be kind.
But she shivered

at the thought of being
confined, rotting slowly
disintegrating with or without me.
I could see her imagining

her lack of departure
her failure to die well, even
her failure as a wife
in flames of some disloyalty.

She did not call me
a stinking materialist
a shit Buddhist
a poor form of bacteria—

nothing like that.
We just stood in the hallway
fighting tears
before we made the bed.

Swallowing her self-reproach
I tried to sleep with her.
I dared not cling—
ending up in the spare bed.

3

This morning—
I am holding on
to the love I saw in her.

I am clinging to the prospect
of one day making
ashes of the mind.

I can see, in theory
her ashes mingling
with my ashes

in a time and place
to which others can attend.
Or, at the very least

half of her urn
being poured there
on my earthly place

her other half
at whatever time
joining the outgoing tide.

Will that suffice?
Is there sufficient
boundlessness in that?

Belatedly, After Sad News, Chewing Things Over

I try to look—its eyes of darkness.
I try to speak—a mouth of silence.
—T'ao Ch'ien

1

It takes ages to wake from the dream
of killing and being killed. Was that you?

Final slumbers, heavy and erotic.
Now, in the spring garden reading T'ao Ch'ien

a man might kid himself—
think well of immortality! Foolish again!

Truth is, he is becoming tongue-tied.
Even before the organ is dead

and lies in his mouth like a slug
after heavy rain, he is chewing on silence.

Soon, as much as he might try otherwise
he is dumb before his wife.

When she speaks to him tenderly
it must suffice to bow.

2

T'ao Ch'ien thought much of his wine cup.
When on the higher deck, leave the shot-glass measure

down in the long grass.
At dusk the birds return in pairs.

Old friend, the bat, flits and disappears.
Stuck for words, only a chant will do.

Swallow the sun as it drops without a sound.
Eat the stars as they fall into your lap.

Then, having heard no call
she arrives in the chair beside yours.

3

With a wide view of the bay
you might recover your life again. As if.

Without speaking, you can have
Everything else you want. Don't argue.

Look at the storm clouds
scudding over the city, streaming away north east.

If you are here on New Year's Eve
the fireworks will explode, without another war.

Gallahs among the eucalypts— raucous and repetitive.
Tongues clack clack, like nuts in broken shells.

Count your blessings. Ask yourself—
what more did I have to say? In any case.

Stylish: First Day of Spring

There they are, swimming again.
How can you not notice?

She is wearing the same bikini
with the sag her bum forgives.

And he is a bit thicker than the crummy
base notes he plodded on with

during the winter that seems
to have vanished like your cough.

But they are in. Without pausing
or shuddering, they slid into the calm grey waters

setting out to swim the length of the black stonewall
even as they knew they could not.

You are going to have to give it another go yourself.
You are still on the planet so that means

breathing your way across the lovely
stretch of time becalmed, its silver ripple

and tidal stretch. Today, the school of salmon
have gone, the dolphins and cormorants with them.

It would be just you (once the others have dressed and left).
Maybe today, after you get the mower serviced

you can drop by the surf shop, get yourself
one of those vests to keep in the warmth—

shark grey, perhaps, with a blue trim.
That's the go.

After Reading David Hinton's *Ching*

You come to the phrase *wild bounty*
and the dragons in you stir
with Root Branch rising
to join
she who tickles your fancy, Lady She-Voice.

Now you are blood arising
a single one
the kind ascent
amazed at the tropical effect
of a single phrase:
it sets you off like a goblet of pheromones.

Who needs 'Nothing'
(that 'Emptiness')?
No such thing is among the ten thousand things.
What there is is in the wind pipes
is ash in the gullet
ash on the mind.

The right way to die:
Root Branch and LSV in furious flamenco
swooning in fusillades
flame's hiss and crackle.
Only the rain knows, thunder
and lightening knows…

Tzu Jan/Self-Ablaze

On entering
or being in

early spring sea—
no grief at
icy bones!

Think marrow
deepest heat or
tzu jan, self-ablaze!

Summer 2020
Four Poems

Revelations

This morning
miles from Events
(too obvious, and heart-wrenching
to mention again before bedtime)

an Apparition! The wet lawn!
Grass that gleams.
Garden furniture that looks charred
but smells of new rain.

Each drop from fresh sky
falls on temples of mind
as if to baptismally treat burns
crimes against Mother Earth.

There is no healing.
There'll be little more rain.
This morning's just a reminder
of the Summer of the Koan—

questions arising from the Great Clod
are just openings, one into the other
like Lotus on pools of fire
petals drifting into flames.

And the lean woman
her Goat on a leash
saunters towards the Great Leader
proclaiming he's neglected her God.

And it's all there, in the writing.
See the character for Fire.
It hardly differs from Water.
Barely a stoke between them.

The Last Post

Next day, there's bitterness
on the tip of the tongue.

No damned question about it.
Ash.

As if you have spent
the night with your face in a grate.

But don't exaggerate. After all
you have tasted it before.
In Darjeeling, on the stairway to Heaven

the people cook on coal-fire stoves
pumping their night air with bitterness.
And no one much worries there.

Here, what must have happened
is that yesterday evening's Easterly
which caressed and cooled your face

as you stood on the pier
later took on the burden of elsewhere.
Now you can at last to some extent, share.

Time alone will tell
the volume of blackened breath
your own system can bear.

And speaking of volume
a woman on the radio announces
that on waking this morning in her town

further along the coast at the front
she gasped at the eerie silence:
only one bird, a magpie, could be heard.

Go sing to it, you say to yourself.
Stand outside in sooty truth.
The bitterness is cold

but it's not too late.
not too late.
The army's in reserve.

Straw Dogs

In our thatched hut on a meager lane, I'd
eluded illustrious guests. But a midsummer

wind hit, wild and steady, and suddenly
houses and trees— everything caught fire…

—T'ao Ch'ien, *6th Month, Wu, Year of the Horse: July 418*

Wherever you look, Great Leaders
are loosing their grip, reaching for
assassinations, missiles, kidnappings, trials.

Everyone wishes they knew the way
the wind's blowing, which way the fire's coming
or going, the extent to which to accuse

ourselves, *take it out* on ourselves.
T'ao Ch'ien writes of his 'lone spirit', 'at home in idleness'
'pure and enduring, a singular

element unto itself and harder than jade'…
If only. T'ao Ch'ien ends up watering his garden.
So what to do from here?

An essay? Another never-ending essay?
If I start I myself might never end.
Essays can barely keep up with the wars we are in:

skies light up with sentences going down
words explode for the dead all around
everyone you know is speechlessly thinking

of birds, love, trust, children, virtue, collectives, *inward training*
pyres, prayers, stampedes – the real work still to be done
with the old words among embers. Imagine—

a garden hose, its rose, its vital spirit
becoming a joining of forces. 'Listen–
it's never ending analysis that wounds us.'

Kind Of: Memo to Greta

Welcome today's rain
it comes from the Coral Sea.
It has passed over the bleached reefs
opening itself up
all the way here to the south

arriving as a kind of welcome totality—
flooding neurosis, offering a kind of relief to chronic fatigue.
Kind of kind of kind of, the way
vomiting after thinking is a relief.
Vital Breath chokes on itself in the tropics of rain.

My books are moldy and still I consult
the old character for *mysterious darkness*...
But so what? So eat your heart out
you Black Hole you. Editing is just
another word for picking through one's vomit.

Greta, dear girl, poor thing, your mother sings
because it's all she can do. She does not sing for you.
Like it or not, she hears each and every instrument in the orchestra pit.
Some notes as sharp in her throat as razor blades—hard to admit, yes
as she rises, like a solitary plover, into her 'superpowers'...

Greta, the other day on YouTube I saw you say
'I'll see you on the streets'
and you brought, at last, tears to my eyes.
You said it with that sweet, crooked smirk
and once again I thought of Amrozi's smile

and was terrified, parentally so
I am sorry to have to tell you.
But the tears were there, like the rain.
They were a relief, kind of, as if they came
to wash off ignorance and shame.

Earth Mother sings to make herself happy.
Earth Mother falls silent with the birds.
Earth Mother will drown in the flood.
Earth Mother is shrill in the rapids.
Earth Mother falls down when she quietens.

The Good in Moonlight

For Kynan Sutherland

The painter
a part-time carpenter and builder

—O would that he had one life
like the trimmed nature of an excellent brush.

But he does not
and that is good, too.

The other truth is that
he drives sweetly between the forest trees
spotting the good timber.

With each vista he loves
shadows and timbered shoulders
as easily as his children climb onto his.

Who would cut them down?
Who wants more than to see kids grow?
The shifting, limited hues of paintings ensure their becoming.

Here is a lovely turn in the road.
You have to pause as you curve to ascend
the bare shape with hardly a fence.

It's there to be what it is in moonlight.
The bend of a road with an open face—
drained of colour, presenting as virtue.

Notes

Epigraphs:
Hugh MacDiarmid, *The Revolutionary Art of the Future, 23*
Yang Wan-Li is cited in David Hinton's anthology, *Classical Chinese Poetry*, 420.

Two Poems to Songs
The songs were written by Willie Nelson (sung by Patsy Cline) and Randy Newman respectively.

By the Shore of Swan Bay
That Beautiful Black Horse recounts an event in 2013 at the gate to Swan Island, Queenscliff, the site of the secret military base, headquarters of the Australian Secret Intelligence Service, where the events in *Unspeakable Heroes* took place in 2014.

Murmured Conversations is the title of an annotated translation of *Sasamegoto*, a treatise on poetry by monk Sinkei (1406–1475), translated by Esperanza Ramirez-Christensen.

The Last European, Berger's essay 'Undefeated Despair' is in *Hold Everything Dear: Dispatches on Survival and Resistance*, 7.

A Few Cheap Poems
The concept of *'Unborn'* resolved a fundamental problem for Zen Master Bankei: after years of pondering what a Confucian teacher (on the recommendation of his mother) brought to his attention in the *Great Learning*: that 'the way of great learning lies in clarifying bright virtue'. Thus Benkei's route to the Buddhist notion of 'original face'—what might be sought in ourselves, and in each other. What I could not quite get into this poem, however, was a vision of a truly virtuous 'nursing home'—where, in each doorway, you could glimpse people leaning into each other's essence.

Alice Springs Poems
Hidden Valley is a slum camp north of the range in Alice Springs, where the Hayes Family live, the Native Title holders of the town. Yeperenya (Caterpillar) is the supermarket in Alice Springs; 'life is a joyous thing with maggots at the centre' is cited by the anthropologist WEH Stanner, who wrote of the Dreaming as 'the poetic key to reality'. In the Aranda emu dance a man dangles a wooden tjurunga around his neck, signifying his heart. 'Medicine Story', *Papunya: A Place Made After the Story*, Geoffrey Bardon and James Bardon, introduction by Paul Carter, 305.

Dear Les was written a few months before the death of Les Murray. *His brilliance is in our blood* is from 'The Moon Man' in *On Bunyah,* 60.

Badly Mothered, Blazing Chaos. The epigraph, slightly edited, is in Sam Hamill's *Basho's Ghost*, 73.

Chuang Tzu in Seoul: 'Boundless Roaming' and 'Making Things Equal' are the first and second chapters of the Chuang Tzu. 'The Dictator' refers to Chun Doo-hwan and his notorious massacre of democracy activists in 1980; 'Ting the Cook' is the subject of a poem in Chapter 3 of the Chuang Tzu.

Tzu Jan—a central concept in ancient Chinese, means 'self-so', made of two characters: one the sign for 'self', the other 'what is so of itself.'

Summer 2020 cites *The Selected Poems of T'ao Ch'ien*, translated by David Hinton, 63 and 42. *Kind Of: Memo to Greta* draws on the Thurnberg family memoir, *Our House Is on Fire*; *Scenes of a Family and a Planet in Crisis.*

The Good in Moonlight draws from a painting, 'Moonlght Flats', 2020, by Kynan Sutherland.

Acknowledgements

Most of these poems appear for the first time, some in different versions, by editors at *Arena* ('The Last Eurkopan', 'Ambassador', 'The Gusts', first published as 'The Real Truth', 'Summer 2020'), *The Australian* ('Mister Lincoln or Camp David', 'Unspeakable Heroes'), *Antipodes* ('Chuang Tzu in Seoul'), *Meanjin* ('The Glove', 'Kind Fire'). Patient friends were subjected to various drafts, helping to keep my spirits afloat: Graham Bird, Godwin Bradbeer, Justin Clemens, Rai Gaita, Kieran Finnane, Susan Fealy, Philip Huggins, Paul Kane, Richard Murphet, Rod Moss, Ian Roberts, Kynan Sutherland, Richard Tanter, Ian Wedde.

And thanks go to Godwin Bradbeer, grandly generous, for the cover image, *Self Portrait as a Wasp* (detail), chinagraph, pastel, and silver oxide on paper, 2009.

And to my son, Joe, for the design of the book; and to my wife, Rose Bygrave, who brought, as ever, all of her intelligent love to bear.

BARRY HILL has worked as a journalist and psychologist in Melbourne and London. He has been writing full-time since 1976 and is the author of many works in several genres, including a libretto performed in 'The Studio' at the Sydney Opera House in 2004. He has written widely for radio, and his short fiction has been frequently anthologised. He's had residencies in Alice Springs, Rome, Kyoto and Santiniketan, Bengal, and is possibly best known for his major works *Broken Song* (Knopf 2002) and *Peacemongers* (UQP 2014). He is a former Education Editor of *The Age*, Poetry Editor of *The Australian,* and a Post-Doctoral Fellow from the University of Melbourne. He lives in Queenscliff, near the Heads of Port Phillip Bay, looking out across the sea towards Tasmania and the Antarctic. He expects his next book to be called *The Tao on Cloudy Bay*. He is married to the singer/songwriter Rose Bygrave.

www.ingramcontent.com/pod-product-compliance
Ingram Content Group Australia Pty Ltd
76 Discovery Rd, Dandenong South VIC 3175, AU
AUHW020135130726
429791AU00003B/125

9 781925 98480